The Language of Emotions

Nicole M Scott (CoCheil)

The Language of Emotions

A Poetry Anthology

Literary Masterpiece Publishing | Ohio

Published in the United States by Literary Masterpiece Publishing
The Language of Emotions

First Printing, 2016

ISBN -10: 0-9974880-0-X
ISBN-13: 978-0-9974880-0-5

Library of Congress Control Number: 2016905840

Printed in the United States of America
Ohio

Literary Masterpiece Publishing

"Painting is poetry that is seen rather than felt, and poetry is painting that is felt rather than seen."

— Leonardo Da Vinci

Foreword...

The Language of Emotions is a sincere and heartfelt anthology written by Nicole Scott. The book delves into experiences of love, mostly of romantic and passionate natures. What I like most about the collection is the way in which it is written with a lens of love. It achieves a specific effect, giving the reader the impression that the author is a deep and eternal lover, and can never really run away from her feelings.

I found that the lyrics captured feelings truthfully and beautifully. Love at times makes one fragile and amazed at one's own vulnerability. At other times, it's strong and secure. Often, poems are rich in imagery and in delving into loving depths of the soul. As a poet myself, I find some overlap with Nicole's style and applaud her eye for beauty and sincerity. There are also philosophical questions on the fantasy of love, and it is clear the author wants to feel that her experiences are all real, and not simply fantasy.

Fascinatingly, some poems are written from the masculine perspective, and this adds variety and intrigue to the progression of the collection. It is done in a very subtle way and what I take from this is a most sacred and spiritual fusion of masculine and feminine, where the lover experiences love from the other's point of view. I highly recommend this book to anyone interested in simple verse and straightforward but beautiful poetry on love, which is sincere and thoughtful. It is definitely a piece of work many will identify with and appreciate since the themes are universal.

Reviewed By Nandita Keshavan for Readers' Favorite

For Nevaeh

Table of Contents...

Forbidden
Love

Thunderous clouds linger like nightmares fraught and foil

Trying to suppress the sunset; diffuse the glow for

happiness' spoil

A sigh pampered across time at hence

Blights of rhyme and reason bright as future's tense

Spent to cosset for care to cease as all seems weary

Like a treasure; true thoughts and ideals forbiddenly

buried

As a breeze touches the face as the hand of God

Heed the concern as fraught is odd

Out of place, no pace, no face, for feelings succumb

Present tense of disillusion as there's no place to run

Thunderous clouds linger like nightmares fraught and foil

The sunset shines through the darkness embraced by seeds planted

in happiness' soil...

The Masterpiece

Art; whispers to the soul a language only translatable to the heart

A proposition to paint you; without the colors to start

Representative of personality and poise: a direction

Which medium was proper; an endearing question

Intrigue and mystery, a quiet sexiness that thoughts provoke

Like a beautiful painting, intense emotions and desires evoked

Envisioning the painting in my dreams, but my hands unworthy to touch the surface

This masterpiece; I wanted a master's piece as visions of mistakes made me nervous

Could I ruin it all from rushing one stroke of my brush?

Could I ruin it all from relinquishing the color of my touch?

All imperfections perfectly perfect in the eyes of this beholder

Subjective to most, but to the artist, a piece that outdoes the skills of its sculptor

Falling in love with the work that basically unfolded itself

Putting my name on a piece these hands never felt

Bright colors, earth tones, or monotones, which are reflective of you?

You're a mixed media work; one medium could never capture the complete essence of you

A painting that came into existence practically on its own

A work of art I'm proud of and want admired by the young and old

Art; whispers to the soul a language only translatable to the heart

By trying to paint you, you transformed me into your latest work of art...

Time and Space

Voices echo as silent cries 'tis sense...

Alas the resonance of forevermore at resilience bent

A luxury yet curse unaffordable to most

Life's incubator; an invisible womb silently whispering like a ghost

'Tis endless times amount to a moment's grace

Almost infinite in the mind outside the realm of time and space

A sigh representative of a pause in time...

Frozen still an illusion that deceived thine mind...

Yet the fantasy felt so real; breathlessness

As it was imagined, a love beyond heaven sent

Dissipated like the deep fog in early spring...

A halo envisage as the heart impulsively crowned thy queen

 Aloof; surrendered to a forbidden spell

That rests only in the mind as the soul awaits to exhale...

A fallacy only spoken amongst the midst

A reality if a Genie could grant one wish

'Tis endless times amount to a moment's grace...

A treasure of the mind as envisioned in a moment of time and space...

Missing You

The stroke of my brush, a masterpiece I forbade

Echoing sounds of water splattering against the window pane

Insanely driven into a state of solitude

Bright colors fill the canvas attempting to establish the mood

Of gestures, reminiscent of how minds silently converse

Like a magnet, souls actually thirst

For a sentence, one mention, so unduly true

The soul speaks through the canvas, a power, even words cannot do

The stroke of my brush, a masterpiece that takes days

Echoing the sounds of my soul as sunlight beams through the window pane...

Fear of Love

From a moment's passing, sprinkled onto my heart like morning dew

It's difficult to fathom how quickly I've fallen for you

Like I'm under a spell without an antidote.

I feel like I can stand in the rain without getting soaked

Your words mesmerize and intrigue as my hands paint your soul

Your presence has me telling stories left untold

Many of nights, I desperately tried to shake what I feel

Terrified; could this be real?

So intensely passionate; it runs so deep

Breathlessness as I see your face in my sleep

To runaway?

I did, but I have to let this be

Only through love are we truly set free

Can't Let Go, Forevermore

Rantings of a drunken whore

Beating at my chamber door

My mind says, "Go away",

But my heart simply can't ignore

I implore then open the door

To a tear stained face and a silent cry

No matter what she did, I can't take the look of pain in her eyes

Her soul is cracked as I wonder who did it

As emotionally drained as I am, I have to help her fix it

I know she can't do it on her own

Like a sponge, I absorb her emotions, and it's so strong

Sucking and sucking that pain out of her into me

Needing extra sleep 'cause it's literally draining me,

But I can't let go

I can't turn anyone away

I'm obsessed with the word "save"

Rantings of a drunken whore

Beating at my chamber door

My mind says, "Go away",

But my heart simply can't ignore

This heart of mine is my curse...

Forevermore.

Goodbye Love

That sparkle in the eyes that glisten like stars sprinkled against the black canvas of the night sky like gemstones.

The sound of that voice as beautiful as the melody of rushing waters echo in my ears when alone

That smile that is reminiscent of the bright glow from the sun; almost too beautiful to behold

A soul that is similar to, but is different, from yet speaks the same melody as my soul

An unexplainable balance of two hearts and two minds

One passive, one aggressive but like the ying-yang they bind

A balancing act creating a distance at hence

A connection that is both past yet present tense

An unforgettable-ness that both dismiss in time

Suspended within different eras, wants and needs, ideals, and rhyme

We silently speak to each other; a call we can feel within our thoughts

Although everything we had, thought we had, actually didn't have, is lost

Within the realm of time and space, floated away like a cold front

Torrential rains, crashing lightning, even sunny days as confusion on both sides rest at the forefront.

Some things are unexplainable, sometimes inconceivable, but some-times the thing to do is often left unspoken

You spoke a language only my soul could transcribe more potent than your average love potion

Everything, including the mundane, happens for a reason even if the reason doesn't make sense

Nothing lasts forever, so we must cherish everything for the short space that it's sent

Sometimes the most difficult yet stupidest thing to do is walk away and say goodbye

But you leave when your heart wanted you to stay due to not trusting how you feel, stubbornness, and pride

You would give anything for another chance to be hypnotized by those almond-shaped dark brown eyes

Trying to shake off what you feel because the distance is burning you inside

That sparkle in the eyes that glisten like stars sprinkled against the black canvas of the night sky like gemstones

Will forever stain my heart, intrigue my mind, playing a melody on repeat to my soul, imprinted in my memory every night my eyes close.

Broken Hearted

Silence, yet I can hear the wind blow

On deaf ears falls the voice of my soul

Wanting to remain in the background, yet at the same time, yearning to be heard

Thinking too much; over analyzing – something, for a philosophical thinker, that's absurd

Theoretically speaking, metaphorically creeping, inside of my own mind

Not wanting to believe what I hear or see like a pause in time

So many speak, preach, relief but hardly ever mean what they say

On my knees for days I pray wondering if this rain will cease or spray

Either way, it doesn't matter to me because I've grown numb

Like a light switch, if I so choose, I will not succumb

To the tyranny; I have no choice to face and deal

To the point where I'm on autopilot; I'd rather not feel

A thing regardless of what it is or what it brings

My soul speaks a language not many can decipher like an invisible screen

Saying exactly what I mean but have folks misinterpreting because they don't understand what I mean

Reading in between lines that haven't been written

Speaking words that for some seem forbidden

A silent yet powerful force that none can deny

A person whose tears you will never see come from their eyes

Silence, yet I can hear the wind blow

As God quietly repairs my soul...

Falling in Love

Feeling the warmth of the sun massaging my cheek on a rainy day

Hearing birds chirping harmoniously on a bitterly cold winter day

Feeling cool breezes molest my body during the desert's heat wave

Hearing nature sounds like a beautiful symphony that goes on for days

Feeling your touch from a simple thought

Hearing your voice in my head brightening my day in ways I never thought

Feeling near you although you're far away and can't be next to me

Hearing the song of your heart and loving the melody

Feel...

Hear...

Feel...

Hear...

Seeing the invisible silhouette of

Hearing the silent voice of

Feeling the illusory touch of...

...falling in love...

Finding Herself Again

Rain forcibly smacking against the window pane

Lightning striking the earth igniting flames

Thunder roaring loudly across the skies

Reminiscent of the pain in the back of a woman's eyes

Waterfalls calmly crashing down

The peaceful wilderness, like music, full of sounds

Beautiful flowers bloom symbolic of birth

Reminiscent of a woman realizing her worth

Boulders crashing down as the mountain moves

The tears of angels quietly soothe

Volcanoes erupt with energy as lava poureth

Reminiscent of a woman that restored her courage

Stars glisten in the night speaking volumes

The moon smiles at mother earth as her magnet calls him

The clouds show the beginning and the end

Reminiscent of a woman dreaming again.

Sunlight reflecting across the open seas

Seeing the rhythmic laughter of the leaves on the trees

Tropical winds caressing the body so gracefully one can't get enough

Reminiscent of a woman in love...

Wounded Soldier

Wounded soldier

Keep your head held high

It's not a sign of weakness; it's okay to cry

Holding emotions inside will lead you to an early grave

Time heals all wounds starting today

Stop holding onto memories of a daunting past

The pain in your heart will not last

Patch yourself up for those wounds will heal

Pick yourself up and get back out on that field.

Wounded soldier

Keep your head held high

All wounds heal; don't let the fire burn out of your eyes...

So Long

So long, so long,

Is in the song

And in the way you're gone

So far yet near

Giving me courage yet fear

Causing such pain yet erasing tears

Memories of a past that's also present

Both dreadful yet pleasant

A smile reminiscent of heaven

Sigh

Making me smile yet sigh

Causing me to realize

Sometimes it's best to deny

So long, so long

Is in the song

And in the way you're gone

But I will remain strong

Blindness

Blindness...

I can close my eyes...

But my heart still sees

I can close my mind...

But my heart still sees...

I can close my ears...

But my heart still sees

I can turn my back...

But my heart still sees

My heart is like a wild animal that not even I can tame

Trying to get my mind to override my heart feels like with myself I'm playing a dangerous game

Feelings flowing deeper than the deepest trench drowning me as I'm prevented from reaching the surface...

So I can breathe...

The thought or possibility of being hurt doesn't even make me nervous...

A repetitive seed...

That I plant yet nothing grows

I'm blind to repercussions even if my mind knows

Blindness...

I can close my eyes...

But my heart sees

I can close my mind...

But my heart sees

I can close my ears...

But my heart sees

I can turn my back...

But my heart sees

Drowning me in the deepest trenches of my own emotions

Unable to breathe or to focus

Trying to escape by using my mind

Although my heart sees...

...she remains blind

The Rose; Thorns and Thistles

Every rose has its thorns,

but every thorn is not the only latch on the stem of that rose

...thorns & thistles...

The prickles of the thistle;

more painful than thorns...

...grown wild; untamed...

Concealing secrets...

therein contains the likeness of fruit

...delicious; vulnerable...

The thistle is armor

...grows slowly...

A hassle to get through the prickles to the fruit...

Some people appear to be simple roses...

...beautiful...

A compliment to anyone's garden...

...a must have...

...challenging upkeep...

        ...captivates...

With thorns attached to their stems...

The admirer dismounts each thorn...

...one by one...

Perceiving the rose as safe...

...prepared to mount in the garden...

A masterpiece...

Pampering and giving it care to keep it bloomed...

...beautiful...

In the center of that beautiful rose...

...lies a thistle...

The prickles of the thistle are painful...

...yet...

...one by one...

...removing...

...hurts then heals...

...hurts then heals...

Making you wonder...

Why did I desire that rose in the first place?...

...sigh...

You've come too far...

...one by one...

...removing...

That glimpse of beauty within...

Your burning desire motivates...

...hurting and healing...

...hurting and healing...

...that glimpse...

...that ideal...

That beauty you must...

    ...sigh...

You have to call your own...

...removing...

...one by one...

...hurting and healing...

...hurting and healing...

...sigh...

You've dismounted every single prickle...

    ...accomplished...

      ...your prize...

You deserve it...

The fruit appears delicious; loving...

A fairy tale...

...a must have...

...sigh...

Impatient to try...

    ...disappointed...

...bitter sweet...

Isn't fruit after all...

...another thistle...

Your eyes have deceived your senses,

as you removed the thorns & thistles...

they latched onto you...

...the self-deceit...

The rose failed you...

Transformed you into a thistle with thorns along your stem;

Mounted the soil with your prized rose...

Refusing to rid the ideal...

Ruining your own garden...

Your desired rose dismounted you in the process...

...thorns & thistles...

      ...removing...

In search of fruit that does not exist...

...hurts then heals...

...hurts then heals...

...a continuous cycle...

The garden quickly barrens...

Nothing grows...

Fertile soil;

the love essential to growth...

      ...none is left...

Only thorns & thistles...

      ...of two souls afraid to give up...

      In loyal...

Not love...

To uproot?...

      ...it's better...

Less is more...

More is less...

Piercing the carnation...

The one you bypassed for the beauty of the rose...

...sigh...

In full bloom...

    ...sigh...

In full splendor...

    ...sigh...

More beautiful now than it's ever been...

    ...sigh...

Realizing...

You should have complemented your garden with the carnation...

    ...roses?...

        ...SIGH!...

    ...thorns and thistles...

        ...hurts then heals...

Constantly removing...

Until the soil...

    ...becomes desolate.

Self-Inflicted Wounds

Self-inflicted wounds from emotions you don't want to erase.

Memories, all there's left, as you yearn for another taste.

Get over it; you have to get over it but choose not.

Even though it's over, you're left with so many good thoughts

That thing, that fling, made you realize what you deserve

Settling for less for so long and they could not quench your thirst.

Losing interest so quickly it's amazing.

Suspended in one moment in time through a daydream.

Hoping you'll be blessed again with someone whose heart is compatible with yours.

Not trying to live in a moment but not ready to close that door

An eye opening experience you'll take with you for the rest of your days.

You smile every time you think of it, and you are forever changed,

In the most positive ways conceivable.

You learned to be you again and the feeling of such freedom is unbelievable.

Self-inflicted wounds from emotions you don't want to erase

Memories, all there's left, thinking of them still brings a smile to your face.

Reminiscence

Reminiscence...

Visions that creep in at night

Opposite the room, the sun lights

The darkest creases of souls

To behold...

To consume...

To be consumed

By hearts with closed rooms

No way in, peering through a crack

Seeing a set of eyes that momentarily wink back

Hollowed from inside out

From a stare, as silence is a shout

The heart speaks

As the words, echo away out of reach

But visions still creep in at night

Opposite the room, the sun lights

The silhouette of a glimpse of love...

...Reminiscence

When We Meet

I've already spread my wings, and I'm preparing to take flight

But the wind isn't blowing and weather conditions simply aren't right

Patiently waiting to hear a familiar song

I am butterfly, but I always return home

In my dreams, I can see your silhouette without a face or a name

My fantasies haunt me as I yearn to see your face

Is your beauty internal?

Wondering if your love is beautiful and eternal

Like an inferno, burning for me and only me

Are you the vision behind my dreams?

Are you the wind beneath my wings?

Pushing me, blowing me, encouraging me to soar

Holding me up, bringing out the best in me, and helping me open doors

I've already spread my wings, and I'm preparing to take flight

One day we'll meet and change each other's lives...

Definition of Love

The definition of a love?

Like the blind leading the blind

Love has no eyes, no mind

Just an intense emotion that is felt more than spoken

Indescribable and only behind the scenes spoken

Making love is so powerful because the body speaks

Words without words as two hearts speak

To one another, a silent language full of passion

To be in love, is another form of madness.

Fires ablaze burning deep, so deep

Reality becomes better than the dreams we have when we sleep

Addictive, it's so addictive like an illegal substance

When things go bad, wondering where the love went

The definition of a love?

Like the blind leading the blind

Depends on the perception a person has in their mind...

Orgasm

A power surge of energy through the gentle gliding of flesh

An indescribable presence fluttering throughout the essence

An intensity of passion unto the spiritual in scenes

Frame by frame; inch by inch

Passion so deeply imbedded yet freed from the soul

Intensity as rhythms in motion

An orchestra only heard by two

Chirping along into one dance

A breeze that tingles down the body in waves

Rippling the warmth in tense

Intensity as rhythms in motion

Frame by frame; inch by inch

An indescribable presence rippling throughout the essence

Until it's released...

The Breeze

A breeze...

Like a summer's passing through the hollows of time

Whispering ambiguities as intangible as a reason

The heat of the flame feeling twice removed

Surrendered...

It surrendered; we surrendered...

The fantasy for a veracity too unfeigned for the imagined

Fluid; like the sounds heard when submerged underwater

Gasping for air although we're already above the surface

Once ignited flames within from a simple glance

Torching the sheets with our rhymes and rhythms

Inexplicable how the storm clouds emerged

Removing the heat and dousing the flame

Burned out; it burnt out...

Leaving smoldering coals willing to reignite in present or future tense

The winter never felt colder

Remembering the summer before its passing

The air was so crisp to inhale

The warmth from the sun penetrated my essence

Sigh; I sighed...

My heart skipped a beat as my soul smiled

Whispering ambiguities as intangible as a song

Like a winter's passing through the hollows of time

The breeze?...

...I still feel it...

Deceitful Heart

Sighs from within

Feeling the breeze that never seems to descend

Hearing that melody that plays on repeat

One dance; that lost chance that haunts me in my sleep

The "what if's" died a long time ago

Forbidden to my soul, but I have to let go

To welcome another that's a piece of work

Once loved someone so bad it literally hurt

I breathed them; thought that it was them I need

And that breeze?

The illusion of love that's as thick and thieves

Sighs from within

Invisible; but tangible from within

Yearning to capture a breeze that doesn't belong to me

Yet welcoming a breeze that sings a song to me

How can my heart be so deceitful?

Thinking I can erase love by loving another is inconceivable

Illogical for this poet at heart

Sometimes cannot tell the difference between the ending and the

start

Recognizes one thing for sure

The heart may mislead but the soul is for sure

There's no rules or precepts for love

In love yet falling in love...

...my heart has deceived me...

The Forbidden Dance

The forbidden dance…

Like a motion that lacks emotion; pure animal instinct

The id meeting conscious awareness without any control

Pure adrenaline matching the mental vision

Hot flashes from hidden burning desires

Needing a cold shower but even that can't tame the body

The mind has locked its target like a missile launcher

Wanting to give your body contorted schisms for the rhythms as we lock eyes

Wanting to connect your soul with mine; for the moment

Let me be the blues in your thighs as we take this thing to spiritual heights

Lust, lust, and more lust; making the mouth salivate

Wanting to make your body tingle every time you think of me

Wanting to make you shiver as your lips quiver and you're left speechless

Nothing but tears drizzling down your face as we embrace

The forbidden dance…

Lingering

Lingering...it just lingered

Like a still wind on a day full of storm clouds

Lingering...left to wonder what's next

And unrequitedness...those unanswered questions

Yet again

no response

Left in limbo...

unsure...

unknowing

just lingering

Lingering...it just lingered

Nothing crueler than being left unsure

Left guessing without a sound answer to provide a solid decision

The decision has been made

No longer will these games be played

No longer will be subjected as prey

No longer will it linger

Left in limbo no more

The questions have been erased

No need for a response

The decision has been made

I'm done

Listen

Listen...

To sounds that seem inaudible

Closed-caption without caption though speaks to the soul

An unconscious level of understanding as emotions evoke

Silence...silence...

Listening to the rhythm of one's heart

Like seeing a portion of a rainbow not knowing if that point is the end

or the start

A seemingly magical covenant no one agreed yet leaves its mark

Listen...

As the eyes close in an unnoticeable sigh

Using your hands to create visual poetry that speaks words folks can't

deny

Emotions flowing deeper than a black hole being expressed as you

prepare to fly

Silence...silence...

A beautiful thing for those that think deeply

Inaudible melodies that almost romantically sing to me

Like an inexplicable connection to God that beeches me

Listen...

Just listen...

Art speaks the language of my soul...

...if you just listen...

Have You Seen Her?

Have you seen her?

That particular woman; a little different from the rest

The type of woman that puts my intellect to the test

Has me questioning yet offers possible answers

A song to my heart and to my soul a dancer

Makes me say, "hmmm...for real though?"

Perfectly "annoying" yet speaks to my soul

Sarcasm; yeah I love it

My rebuttals are so magnificent we'll wind up making a covenant

A power struggle?

Never that; I'm willing to submit most times

As long as she matches my rhythm with her rhyme

Ah! A woman with a dream

Willing to make your life as beautiful as can be

I may not be the most beautiful woman in the world.

But I could make your world beautiful if you were my girl

Have you seen her?

That particular woman; more special than the rest

The type of woman I'd never test...

Just give her all of me...

...and then some for eternity...

Have you seen her?...

Sunrise and Sunset

Sunrise and sunset; both beautiful yet mysterious in its origins from fresh eyes of breathless beauty

Ruled by Venus the goddess of love; to genuinely care is your duty

You perceive the world through the eyes of a gifted child; noticing the love throughout any pain

Silently inspiring the world around you with nothing needed in return; smiles and gratitude are what you are to gain.

Life is so short, precious, and beautiful; a concept you seem to grasp better than most

You can literally feel the breeze in your soul living and enjoying life at the highest dose

Your mystery, beauty, strength, and beyond mesmerizes even the cruelest soul

When you love, you genuinely love, and love hard making it difficult to let go

You're optimistic and positive; a true blessing that lights the dark corners of everyone's soul, but I know you're hurting inside.

A beautiful mind and beautiful face without a big name; smiling with your eyes and positive spirit to conceal what's really going on inside.

You've lost two angels; yet you've gain two more guardians to keep you safe

I wish I could be there to hold you, console you, and wipe

away any tear that may drizzle down your face

The one's you love left a cruel chaotic world for an unimaginable peace; a much better place.

This is not a goodbye; it's an "until we meet again" – one day again you will see their face.

Sunrise and sunset; both beautiful yet mysterious in its origins representative of a new beginning and a new life

You're a strong woman and can take care of yourself, but even at a distance, I'm always here by your side...

I'm praying for you and your family...

Fire

Fire's ablaze, burning within the core; the purest of light

From old coals that's never been ignited; didn't know they could ig-

nite

Illuminating a small corner of my soul

Didn't want to fall in love, so I battled myself losing my self-control

Insignificant to most; magnificent to the host

Trying to extinguish my own flame; choking off my own smoke

"Shake it off, you've gotta shake it off" my inner voice silently screamed

Insignificant; I convinced myself to believe

That I was not an empty shell longing to be filled

Secrets locked away for years would not be spilled

I don't want something that can tangibly be felt; setting me free from

the prison of me

But I was self-deceived

From the moment we spoke, I knew it was meant to be

Moving slowly, carefully, wanting feelings to grow naturally

Shattered heart that reflected a terrible choice

Glued back together by kind words and the sound of a voice

That voice that rings in my ears unto this very day

That voice that has me unable to sleep for days

That voice that ignited my soul

That voice that I let go

Fire's ablaze, burning within my core; so out of my sight

From old coals that's never been ignited; felt weird for them to ignite

Illuminating a facet of my life

Torching my soul as I hear that voice echo in my ears at night

Reminding me of how I returned to the prison of me; my comfort zone

Burning my own heart as the flames blaze on...

A Vision

A vision?

Yes just resting in the back of my mind: a fantasy

From the moment I laid eyes on thee: smitten

Like a story told yet unwritten

Beauty and brains for my eyes have seen the glory

Couldn't imagine anything more perfect for me

Then I awakened the next morning to sunlight beaming on my face

That vision, that fallacy, that fantasy...erased

Like a shadow that can't be viewed in daylight

Only real to me in my dreams when I close my eyes at night

A vision?

Yes just resting in the back of my mind: that endearing crush

From the moment I laid eyes on thee: I knew you were someone I could never touch...

A vision?...

She Is...

She is...

A conqueror, a survivor full of strength from the depths of the valley she's arisen

An aura, a definitively powerful presence with inner beauty as her weapon almost foretold like she was previously written

To be a victor although her life has been an annoying splinter, a thorn stuck in her side

And even with tears staining the back of her eyes everyone can see her pride and the fearlessness in her eyes

A level of courage undefined because she is a woman of great depth and strength

Even when knocked into a black hole she comes out practically unscathed no cuts or tears only dents

That heal, they heal, as she bows her head and kneels; like a song those wounds never last long for sure

Even when she shouts, has her doubts, and bouts of frustration, she knows without God in life she couldn't endure

Alone, she's never alone as long as his majesty loves her and has her back anytime she calls

When the world attacks, and her back is up against the wall, it is he that carries her when she falls

Our lady Yar, great woman of strength but that strength is only defined by he who gives her the confidence to face anything

Better things await as she open her eyes to promise of the gates that remain open 24 hours a day cause that's the reward faith brings

And in the rain she dances and sings because she's made it out of the valley; she's arisen

Because she gives praise for days and believe in the aura that was foretold and previously written

She is...

...a woman of God...

The Illusion

The illusion...

Maybe I'm a bit disillusioned

Wondering if my perception of love is a bit fantastical

Or if the intensity thereof others find inexhaustible

Frightening them due to its abysmal depth

Although passionate, tears are something these eyes have seldom wept

A heart that too kind and forgiving for its own good

Often distrusted for no reason, prejudged, and misunderstood

The illusion...

Maybe I'm a bit disillusioned

Although it may seem like it, my love is not an illusion...

...it's pure...

The Silhouette

Whispers of the mind, obscene yet conceiving

Visions appeasing, pleasing, maybe even self-deceiving

The silhouette that appears in the dark

Completely stark, leaving permanent marks, by surprise easily captures the heart

Radiance surpassing that of an exotic flower

Causes others to cower with the desire to devour

As one remembers down to the minute, every single hour

Past yet present, attempting to evict from the mind

Very little time as we bind, and only in my dreams, mine.

With a smile like heaven and overall beauty that's almost surreal.

The very essence causes the unsuspecting to feel and feel, and it's not a fallacy; the feelings are so real.

The silhouette is actually a butterfly that must spread its wings and fly

Saying goodbye, but not goodbye

In the mind, the silhouette cannot be denied, but on the surface, it's easy to deny.

The desire, the flame, the yearning to replay that game, a love that is difficult to tame yet is tamed.

As thoughts remain and feelings attempt to change, for the silhouette with beauty as its name.

Let Me Please You

Breathe me, need me, please me like no one else can

Tickle my soul with your smile and gently take me by my hand

Show me things I've never seen before

Open your mind to me for that is what I'd like to explore

For me, let your walls down

With me, you'll never fall down

I yearn to make love to you in ways that seem inconceivable

I want our love to be so powerful it seems unbelievable

Two bodies dancing in unison as our souls become one.

Hearts hearing the same melody as being together seems like so much fun.

You tickle my soul with your smile, so why don't you just take me by my hand?

I breathe thee, I need thee, let me please you like no one else can.

Locked in a Dream

Locked in a dream it seems

Where the world is full of beauty, love, and peaceful things

But hate abounds

As homeless people continue to wander around

People drive by with expressions of disgust

Living in a world that's difficult to trust

Feeling the pain of others as if it's your own

Wishing it was safe to let homeless people into your home.

Not turning on the television because the news is too painful

Sitting back helpless as Satan gains more souls.

A world where good people are driven cold

A world where strong people struggle not to fold.

Wishing people would love one another

Instead of stepping on and belittling each other

Reality sometimes is difficult for me to conceive.

I'd rather spend my days suspended in a dream.

I'm locked in a dream it seems

Where the world is full of beauty, love, and peaceful things.

A place where hate cannot be found.

A place similar to how heaven sounds.

I'm Worth It

The feeling like a beautiful sun rise on a Sunday morning

Was so afraid of them, tried to block the emotions from spawning

Didn't trust myself, wanted someone else, and didn't want to hurt anyone

Confused myself in a search for that special one.

Yearning for understanding and acceptance I guess

Always wanting things I can never get.

To my surprise, that special one found me.

And even though I tried to push it away, their love surrounded me

Gave me feelings I projected onto someone else.

Didn't even understand what it was I truly felt.

My eyes beseeched me as my heart deceived me.

How blind I was to ignore the treasure that stood before me.

Unbelievable, how could I have been such a fool?

Inconceivable, to give up on me, they refused.

Haven't felt this way in a long time; so sad.

I'm hoping it's real and not a mere infatuation, but either way I'm glad.

How could someone adore little old me so much?

The adoration, support, encouragement, how could I not be in love?

The feeling like a beautiful sun rise on a Sunday morning.

Dealing with me is no easy task, but it's you I'm wanting.

...but, I'm worth it...

Decode My Heart

At a standstill, as the wind molests my body and the sun attacks while my mind slowly loses focus

My heart speaks volumes, spilling melody after melody, while my thoughts remain unspoken

What my heart says often goes unnoticed because the language is untranslatable to most

A hopeless romantic stuck in a fantasy world yet my heart is unavailable to most

It's difficult to capture my heart, but once you do, it's all the more difficult for me to accept it back

Being with me is like a modern day fairy tale causing those that like chaos to not know how to act

Leaving me in a momentary storm as the rain soaks through to the root of my disappointment

Even without being in love the heart can still suffer the pain and hurt of disappointment

My heart speaks volumes, spilling melody after melody, while my thoughts flow like a monsoon

One day the language of my heart will be translatable to someone whose heart sings the same tune.

Within My Grasp

A shadow, that's the silhouette of my past

Beneath me, beseeched me, nothingness was within my grasp

I gasped as love eluded my heart and only non-chalant-ness resided.

The fear of love and my commitment issues, I could not hide it.

Pushing away love without conscious awareness

Telling myself I don't fear anything yet I feared it

Hurt a lot of people within the wake of my confusion

"Never meant to hurt you" a familiar line I remembered using

When it was stated towards me, it was a dose of my own medicine served directly to me.

By someone whose philosophy is a mirror of who I used to be.

Through them, I truly saw my reflection for the first time.

Making me glad I have changed, learned, and grown over time.

I know who I am, what I want, and what I need.

No longer do I or will I push love away from me.

I am on the path to a wonderful, almost surrealistic life

And one day, I will make someone an excellent wife.

A shadow, that's no longer the silhouette of my past.

Underneath me, beseeching me, the world is within my grasp.

False Love

Those days of love are gone.

Getting hopes up high yet at the end of the day listening to sad love songs.

The most dangerous thing is to be in love with fact of being in love.

Increase dopamine levels in the brain making you feel high like on a drug.

Feels good, surrealistic, and blissful.

But it's only a temporary effect that will f*ck up your mental.

You think you're in love but your more in love with the ideal.

So much so that the feeling seems so very real.

Confusing you while eluding you.

Feeling hurt as the "fake" emotion is moving you.

Sometimes to anger and tears.

Elucidating all of your fears.

Then you decide to close your heart.

Not realizing that you were never in love from the start.

To be in love with the fact of being is love is like an addiction to a drug.

When you find true love, you suddenly realize you were never in love.

You Love Me Not

The wind blows

Solemn

Like a beating heart

Can't be felt or heard unless near

A head upon a chest

Just listen; just listening

To the rhythms

The melody?

Questioning if it matches your own

Head lain upon thy chest

As you hear it

You feel it

A mirror to your own

Yet they are oblivious

The winds blows

Solemn

Like a beating heart whose rhythms are heard from afar

It matches your own

But the melody?

Isn't played for you....

If I Was Your Girl

If I was your girl...

I could never hand you the world

But I could show you the world

In ways you've never dreamed of

And I could make you my world

In a land, where broken promises doesn't exist

In a realm, where painful tears have no place

In a reality, where I may annoy you from time to time

In a relationship, where I will love you beyond death

If I was your girl...

I could never give you the world

But you'd be my world...

...if only I was your girl...

Wide Open

Wide open...

My mind and my thoughts submerged in her

Like a submarine slowly sinking to the bottom of the ocean

So deep; with each moment I sink deeper

An unexplainable chemistry

More beautiful than a nebula

As songs play during the sunset

And trees dance rhythmically to a seemingly inaudible tune

My mind and thoughts submerged in her

So deep; with each moment I sink deeper...

She has me wide open...

The Sun Rises Then Sets

The sun rises then it sets

The beginning of a day and the end of one

Darkness soon approaches after the day has expired

But the beautiful black canvas of the night sky isn't an end

It reflects the glory of God

A promise that a new day is dawning

A new chance for redemption

A fresh new start

But sometimes...

The sun has to set

The day has to expire...

And so does life...

The meaning thereof...

Undefined yet defined in the hearts and souls of folks we "touch"

Although the sun has set for some, the rest of us look forward to the sunrise

To witness the sunrise is a blessing

One in which most take for granted

When the sun sets, most don't pay attention to its beauty nor its significance

And...

When the night falls, folks fall asleep without taking a glimpse of the glory before them

The sun rises then it sets

The beginning of a day and the end of one

So many stars that I love within the heavens

Because they remind me of the ones we've lost

And one day

We shall all meet again...

Want to Make You Smile

I want to make you smile

To the point where you can feel the sun beam upon your face

During a storm with the darkest, gloomiest clouds

Every time you think of me

I want your body to tingle

And for you to crave me and only me

When you close your eyes at night

I want to be the last thought on your mind

And when you awaken in the morning

I want you to yearn to see my face and/or hear my voice

I want a love so deep the marinara trench would envy

Eventually...

One day...

But as of right now...

I just wanna make you smile...

Intense

Intense...

So intense

Like lightning striking from the ground upwards

Like a gusty wind of a tsunami

Like a sunset peaking a mist a storm

So much beauty throughout chaos

A silent presence

That most don't seem to recognize for what it is

A talent that seems to be a shadow not many can see

Within the proper light

Similar to gazing unto the sky for the stars in daylight

Unseen...

Unnoticed...

Unrecognized...

A passion so strong most don't seem to comprehend

An unimaginable strength yet a vulnerability that remains hidden

Like a rainbow that briefly shines during a treacherous storm

Intense...

So intense...

Like lightning striking from the ground upwards

Like the gusty wind of a tsunami

Like a sunset peaking through a storm...

Unseen...

Unnoticed…

Unrecognized…

But…

Throughout it all…

Will never be forgotten…

Intrepid

Intrepid; a fearlessness well known to my being

Trying to relax, but my eyes are unsure of what they're seeing

Dove deep down into the ocean yet haven't crest the soul

Like an iceburg, I'm seeing the surface yet so much is unknown

Intriguing; it intrigues me

An unconscious motivation that precedes me

Unrecognizable to the conscious mind...

...yet real so real in my dreams outside of the realms of time

Intense; yes I'm so very intense

I want to make you feel something every time we kiss

Whether lust or love...

Have a feeling I may never have your love...

But in the meantime...

I'm intrepid; fearless in pursuing you

I should stop myself, but my soul recognizes you

Whether here or there; to or fro; I'm right where I belong

Our souls speak a silent tune and a similar song...

In sense even in tense yet the problem is the tense

An issue with two tired hearts with different "perceptions" at hence

Still reeling from past pain; can we heal each other?

Put a bandage on the wounds and lean on one another?

Intrepid; a fearlessness well known to my being

I'm an Aries, my eyes recognize exactly what I'm seeing...

...and I'm going after it...

...win, lose, or draw....

Breathe

Breathe...

Just breathe...

Pay attention to the sound of your heart

The rhythm has a reason

Listen...

Just listen...

To how it thumps

The rhythm has a reason

Breathe...

Just breathe...

Inhale the hidden melody

The rhythm has a reason

Listen...

Just listen...

Beats faster with every thought

The rhythm has a reason

Breathe...

Just breathe...

Stop dismissing your heart

Focus on the reason behind the rhythm...

Now just breathe...

Deeply Woven

Deeply woven...

To the point where some drown within my essence

Or dismiss it entirely...

Intense...

My intensity is as deep as the ocean

All that I am has drowned the both of us into the depths of the Mari-

nara

A place where light isn't supposed to exist yet I illuminate you

And you warm the dark creases of my soul in the coldest waters

A love that's complicated yet simple

Flowing deep into the core yet barely touches the surface

An unpredictability that defies everything that makes sense

An unexplainable chemistry that will never be forgotten

But...

I must swim to the surface to allow myself to breathe

I may have been a victim of a fantasy my mind concocted

My mind is clouded like a thick fog in early spring

Been through so much not really knowing what to think

I know that I need to inhale...exhale...inhale...then exhale again

Slowly struggling to breathe as my heartbeat stops

And my mind grows numb

Deeply woven...

To the point where I've drowned myself...

In an illusion

My intensity is as deep as the ocean...

I feel like I've been drowned into the lowest depths of the Marinara...

Struggling to swim to the surface...

...so I can breathe...

She's Special

She's complicated yet simple

Her heart and soul as fragile as a piece of glass

Yet...

As hard as a diamond

One can scratch the surface

But none can break her

A quiet storm yet a beautiful sunset

A ravaging pitbull

Yet...

As delicate as a flower

A beautiful mess to some

Any work of art is a mess at the core

However...

Folks take a step back

Admire the "mess" and call it "beautiful"

She's complicated yet simple

To some a beautiful mess

But to me?...

She's a masterpiece...

I'm Me

All I can do is be me...

Nothing to prove

Nothing to hide

Just simple old me with a lot of love inside

Aimed towards a special one

I want to give her all of my love

From her hair follicles to her toe nails

From her inner being to the breath she inhales

From soothing her mind to touching her soul

From capturing her heart and never letting go

A vision that feels so real to me

Hoping I'm not deluding my mind with a fantasy

Feelings so strong I can't find the words to explain

As I wait for her, I hope her interest doesn't change

All I can do is be me...

Nothing to prove

Nothing to hide

Just simple old me with a lot of love inside

Aimed towards the woman that makes me feel so alive...

...I love her...

Erotica; The Way You're Desired

Feeling the heat between us while staring into your eyes

Yearning for you to feel with your lips the moisture between my thighs

When I kiss your lips, I love it when you sign a bit

And the look in your eyes makes me yearn for you to lick my southern lips

The blues in my thighs and the thought of you giving my body contorted schisms

For the sexual chemistry is provoked as my body matches your body's rhythms

We grind and grind as the sexual tensions increase

Making you hot as you place your hands on my back digging your nails inside of me

The sighs?

The moans?

Just waiting to release a scream

As I lick up and down, I can feel your body scream

Pleased with me as I bite, kiss, blow, and suck

Your back arcs as we both become the victims of our lust

Going in and out, on top to the bottom, as we intensely stare into each other's eyes

Feeling the tremble of my thighs as I reach towards the sky

The passion and emotion flowing into the depths of the soul that I can't help myself; I'm addicted

Yearning to make you have orgasm after orgasm every time we kick it

Feeling the heat between us while consistently piercing your eyes

When I kiss your lips, I love it when you sigh

Yearning to feel your lips between the moisture of my thighs

I want you to be the one to put a smile on my face and be a blues in my thighs...

Breathlessness

Breathlessness...

When around you, I feel a sense of peace

A calming affect unfamiliar to my being has been released

Rarely even stare at the stars at night

My "lonliness" seems to have disappeared in a sense right before my eyes

Instead of gazing at the stars, I like to gaze at you

...because you are more beautiful than the stars

The black canvas of the night skies offer me a surface for my mind to "paint" you from afar

And the beauty, serenity, and mystery within them is breath-taking at times

...but not as breath-taking as you...

Seeing you today made me feel some type of way; butterflies in my stomach like only you can do

Made me see the angels of heaven as the sky moved the clouds

Although I want you, I don't have much to offer you right now

But in future's tense, I could hand you the world...

Hoping one day you'll wait on me and be my girl

Breathlessness...

When around you, I feel so relieved

For the first time in my life, I'm certain that this is where I want to be

Whether as friends, lovers, or my wife

I want and need you in my life...

Ready To Love

I was ready to love...

To give all of me to that special one

Although I was hesitant...

Not knowing if I had room in my heart for another

The love I had for my past was seemingly inerasable

Didn't think I was capable of letting anyone in

Although I was ready...

Confusion struck my being

Afraid to completely open my heart yet afraid to close it

I was ready for love...

From our first conversation, from the moment we locked eyes...

I clearly saw your soul

Behind your smile, there was pain in the back of your eyes

My mirror; I saw my reflection every time I stared

We couldn't stop smiling at each other

And we both unlocked the diaries of our lives

Undressed our hearts

Wearing loosely held towels around our souls

I yearned for love...

Your reflection and mine were incomprehensibly similar yet differed

Drastically...

We became deeply imbedded; prematurely

The way you looked at me...

I could feel your thoughts; I could feel the emotions you hid

When I looked at you...

I lit a fire in you unfamiliar to your being...

That frightened yet intrigued you...

I surrendered to love...

To hear your voice, brought peace to my noisy world

To make you smile, felt like heaven

I undressed your body

You undressed my soul

When we touched, I could feel your heart

Every time we touched, I snatched a piece of your soul

The intensity was unfamiliar...

So you ran away...

I was reproached for love...

Reeled accusations that belonged to another

My peaceful world became chaotic

Pushed further and further to the edge

Holding on tightly in an attempt to prove myself

But with each tear...

My heart grew colder and colder

As you snatched the towel from around my soul

And smacked me with it

I was ready to love...

I was ready for love...

I yearned for love...

I surrendered to love...

I was reproached for love...

My heart ached to love...

My heart ached for love...

My heart ached...

I was ready for love...

But you weren't

You undressed and shattered my soul...

I've never felt so naked

But now...

I'm fully clothed

And afraid to undress...

My Imagination

Silence...

Breathlessness as I envision you...

My mind wondering into so many different realms

Never met you yet secretly yearn for you

Is this my mind playing tricks on me again?

A mirage that I've seen since childhood

A silhouette without a face or a name

Unconsciously recognizing the attributes

Smitten in a sense

Two souls speaking to each other on incomprehensible levels

Yet...

We haven't even met

Is this just my imagination?

Or...

Do you actually exist?

A joyful fallacy within a false reality

Or...

Am I simply a hopeless romantic in love with the fact of being in love?

Shhhh!

I need to quiet my mind and tame this heart

So open...

So honest...

Too strong and real for the faint hearted

Never learns her lesson for she's open 24 hours a day

Incapable of closing...

But only a few vibes with the rhythms

My heart sends out vibrations not many understand

It is just my imagination?

The inclination of you and me one day?

Silence...

Breathlessness as I envision you...

A victim of my imagination...

Perhaps...

Hopelessly devoted to a mirage...

Those Eyes

Those eyes...

You have those eyes that see

That see some of the hidden parts of me

I don't readily open up to most

It typically takes years for me to reveal the miniscule things that you know

Why I'm so comfortable with you?

Boggles my mind

The key to my heart?

Is stimulating my mind

Most folks can't but somehow you do

Not a minute goes by without thoughts of you

Frightening sometimes because this connection for me is rare

Sometimes when you're not looking I can't help but stare

Wondering what you're thinking and feeling

Reminding me of me and how I can easily hide my feelings

And how most people never know what I'm thinking or feeling

An unpredictable person where routines don't apply

You pierce my soul every time you look into my eyes

Sometimes I feel a sense of nervousness but in a good way

Every single day I hope you have a good day

I'm shocked that my intelligence didn't run you away

Your smile can brighten up the darkest day

Those eyes...

You have those eyes that see

Hoping one day they'll truly see me...

...and love the hidden parts of me...

Nicole M Scott's Biography

Nicole M Scott is thirty seven years old, was born and raised in Dayton, OH, and lives with her eight year old daughter. She is the youngest of her mother's three children, the middle of her father's three children, the only daughter, and first girl on her mother's side of the family. Nicole has been drawing since she was six years old, never had any formal art training other than regular public school art classes; she's completely self-taught. Art has always been a great love and passion for her, and she loves every art form.

Nicole is a member of the following organizations: African American Visual Artists Guild (AAVAG), Dayton Society of Painters & Sculptors (DSPS), National African American Museum and Cultural Center (NAAMCC), Alpha Beta Kappa National Honor Society (ABK), and The Pinnacle Honor Society.

www.cocheilartsgallery.com

Other Books by Nicole M Scott (CoCheil)

Fluid Veracity

Prologue

Loud sirens faded in and out as I went in and out of consciousness. The voices sounded muffled, and I couldn't quite make out what was being said. My eyes opened wide as I stared into the Paramedic's face. His tanned complexion, steel grey eyes, and good looks should have had a calming effect on me as he revealed a false smirk; I noticed the nervousness in his eyes. My mother frantically yelled words I could not hear. Her normally mocha complexion appeared light caramel as her eyes moved here and there almost uncontrollably. The Paramedic placed an oxygen mask over my nose and mouth, and I could feel my heart struggling to beat in my chest; slow and weak. Tears drizzled from my eyes as I spoke silently to God. *Please don't let me die. Lord, I am begging you to please show mercy on me.*

I cried tears of blood as the doors of the ambulance opened. The gurney I was strapped dropped out of the ambulance and rolled away as another set of doors miraculously opened. I was blinded by the abundance of hazy lights that gleamed from the ceiling of the emergency room. The Paramedics surrounded me, running me towards the nearest triage as I attempted to remain calm during this bumpy ride. Every sound was hollow and echoed as my gurney was wheeled into Triage number two. I was alarmed at the amount of people that ran to my aid; doctors, nurses, and others. I couldn't count them if I tried; they kept moving about. My mother held my hand assuring me that I would make it through. She continuously told me to fight. She said, "Fight baby. No matter what, fight."

The doctors switched me from the gurney to the bed as my mother's hand slowly broke away. I turned my head towards my mother, confused because I had no idea what was going on and how I wound up here. I searched silently for answers as I took a glimpse of the gurney. It was full of blood like something off of a gory horror film, only it was real life and not a movie. Panicking, I quickly examined myself; I was covered in blood. The blood was so dark it almost appeared black. With a pair of shears, the doctor cut the clothes from my body. He walked passed my mother as though she was invisible; she was a ghost to him. My eyes locked with my mother's eyes as I noticed, for the first time, how worried she truly was. I could see my reflection in my mother's dark brown eyes and the tears she desperately tried to prevent from escaping.

One of the doctors, a medical student I supposed, asked me for my name. The sound of his voice echoed like it continuously bounced off of a concave wall. I attempted to state my name but was unsure of what name I gave him because I could not hear myself speak. It was like someone tossed me into a black and white closed captioned movie without caption. Everything and everybody were moving in slow motion as I felt a painful pinch in the fold of my right arm. I blanked out then back in.

When I blanked out, I had a flash of a dark-skinned woman but couldn't make out her facial features. She seemed possessed by the way her eyebrows grumbled and her nose flared. The white conjunctivas of her eyes were pink as she had the most hateful expreslsion ike a devil. She was six inches away from my face violently yelling and screaming at me. I paused trying so hard to remember, "Pow!" The sound of a gunshot rang in my ears as it echoed. I remembered. I finally remembered. At this point, I remembered. I leaned up and screamed, "Save my baby. Please save my baby. I am eight months pregnant. Please save my baby." Tears sprayed from my eyes as a bit of reality shed some light on this seemingly nightmarish mystery.

As I cried, panicking, the young doctor injected my I.V. with a clear solution. Almost instantaneously, I was a victim of the surrealism of my mind; trapped momentarily within a dream world. I was unable to distinguish reality from futility.

Was I dreaming? The ambulance ride, the memory of the angry woman, the pregnancy, and my mother finally expressing her emotions; was it real? Is this all in my head? I didn't feel an inch of pain. How could I have forgotten about my baby? It felt like a nightmare, but was it?

The Chosen One

The Father sat on his throne in between the twenty four elders; twelve to his left and twelve to his right sitting beside yet in front of him on a golden thrown that was as clear as glass. The light that he emitted was brighter than 50,000 earthly suns. Any impure life force would immediately die when confronted with the beauty of his glory and the sound of his voice. His voice resounded like a sonic boom with power, authority, passion, and conviction. He glanced at each of the elders then said, "Sound of summon." The elder at each end stood, grabbed the golden trumpet from their stands adjacent to where they sat then blew into them. The trumpets were eight feet long without any keys, constructed of the purest yellow gold with blue satin tassels near the mouth piece. Their stands were light marble with a soft blue velvet covering to protect the precious trumpets. The trumpets sounded as soft as a flute but were as powerful and as loud as a bass drum.

Only seconds after the sounding of the trumpets, Lucifer flew into the Kingdom that sat high on The Holy Mount. He was adorned with precious stones of ruby, topaz, emerald, chrysolite, onyx, jasper, sapphire, turquoise, and beryl set in the purest gold wearing a white robe with a golden sash that firmly held his trident and his sword. Eight feet tall with a muscular, athletic build, his mid-back length hair was so blonde it almost appeared white and his topaz blue eyes were accented well by his thick eyebrows. Not a stitch of facial hair not even a teenage mustache, his almond-shaped eyes quickly pierced the elders as he knelt before The Father with his hands clinched together in front of his chest and his head bowed. He said, "Father, you summoned?"

The Father leaned up in his chair as his light diffused a bit, "Yes. I am creating another kingdom."

Lucifer stood with his head still bowed, "The Earth?"

"Precisely...I have a special assignment for you. You will walk the Earth as my principal guardian cherub."

Lucifer's eyebrows crumbled, "Guardian?...I do not understand Father. I have never been a guardian nor a Cherubim. I'm a Seraphim."

"You are the first, the most beautiful, the wisest, and the most powerful. That is exactly the reason I have chosen you for this special assignment. You will guard the gates of earth and watch over the Cherubim I have chosen."

"The gates of earth?" Lucifer's eyebrows frowned.

"Yes, the portals such as the Bermuda Triangle and others ensuring beings that are not supposed to be there do not come there."

Lucifer stared directly at The Father as he coyly approached the throne. He was the only angel that could ever get that close other than Michael and the other Seraphims; the highest ranking angels that sat amongst God on the thone, "What exactly is this 'special' assignment, hmmm? You desire I become a guardian, yes? Whom will I be guarding?"

The Father stood, "You will guard man."

Lucifer's eyebrows grumbled, "Who?"

"I have created man on the earth from the dust of the ground and given him dominion. I require you ensure man abides by my laws and remain pure for the plan I have for him."

Lucifer snickered, "Cannot be serious. You give a being created from dust dominion over those created by fire? Makes no sense."

"Are you challenging me?"

Lucifer ran his fingers across one of the trumpets resting on their stand; fluttering them, "No...However, I do not understand. The earth is almost as beautiful as I. It makes more sense if I was given dominion over it."

"Do you mock my judgment?"

"Not at all. I am simply stating the facts. Man cannot rule the earth without destroying it. He is too feeble-minded and gullible. He is too weak...and simple-minded. Trust me, you will see. Man will hurt you more than you are willing to realize. Man will bring a wickedness onto the earth as never has been seen before its resurrection."

"All you need to know is that I have a plan, and your part in this plan is to be the guardian cherub on the earth. Do not speak on things which you know nothing about. Dismissed."

Lucifer immediately flew away feeling angry, confused, and irritated. He felt The Father was incompetent to lead. Creating man from dust without any powers was foolish. To create a being so weak and unknowledgeable was the greatest act of stupidity. His plan for the earth? More than likely foolish with an extra side of ignorance in Lucifer's mind.

He landed on a secluded part of the cliff in the Valley of Midst. He stared down at all of the angels as he paced back and forth rubbing his chin with his index finger and thumb. He mumbled, "Makes no sense." He thought to himself, *I am the wisest, wiser than The Father. Simply because he has the power to create doesn't mean he has the competence to lead.*

He stared up at the Holy Mount located in the third heaven. The glory of The Father illuminated the Holy Mount like a beautiful sun inside of a gorgeous nebula. He snarled, "I will be like the Most High. I shine brighter than all the stars in the heavens. I will take the lead. I deserve to sit on that throne. Everyone should bow down, and take orders from me. He is incompetent. Someone must take a stand." He tightly clinched his hands together gritting his teeth.

Uriel appeared beside him wearing his blue and gold armor with his golden shield slung across his back. His big bright emerald green eyes locked with Lucifer's for a quick second. He said, "Hey big brother. Why has the music stopped?"

Lucifer cringed a bit in irritation, "I am so sick of playing music."

Uriel stared at Lucifer in a state of confusion, "But...that's what you were created to do Light Bringer."

"Well, I prefer another purpose...one in which I define," Lucifer crossed his arms and slowly walked around Uriel in a tight circle, "Do you *like* being an Archangel?"

Uriel's eyebrows grumbled in response to the uncomfortable question, "Of...course I do."

"Why so baby brother?"

Uriel paused.

The silence lasted ten seconds before Lucifer spoke again, "Because you are ordered to like it...hmmm?"

Uriel stuttered, "N-n-no...I-I like it because I am a soldier with a special purpose. I like being the angel of 'good news' and doctrinal errors."

Lucifer stopped in front of Uriel snickering, "Good news? What's good about servitude? Hmmm?...allow me to explain. If you could choose to be anything other than what you are, what would it be?"

Uriel paused again. His hands trembled, "Where are you going with this?"

Lucifer stared at Uriel's trembling hand, smirked, patted Uriel on the shoulder then said, "You could never understand. I am truly going to miss how we are. Dismissed."

Uriel stood in silent bewilderment. The Father was the only one that ever said, "Dismissed." Uriel felt in his heart that things were about to change in the heavens. He stared at Lucifer feeling a deep sense of sadness then vanished.

Lucifer pierced the Holy Mount again as he saw Michael flying into the kingdom. His eyebrows crumbled as he spread his wings and flew towards the Holy Mount at the speed of light. Molech saw Lucifer flying toward the Holy Mount, spread his wings then cautiously flew behind him.

Michael flew into the kingdom, knelt, clinching his fists together in front of his chest while bowing his head wearing his purple and gold armor. His sword with three blades shaped like fire hung carefully on his right side in its golden sling case. Michael's almond-shaped medium brown eyes matched his medium brown complexion. He had not a stitch of hair on his head, and his build was athletic, muscular, and strong. He was much smaller than Lucifer in terms of weight and muscle mass yet was still a nice, healthy size.

The Father said, "There is no need to kneel. Stand."

Michael stood as Lucifer hovered outside of the gate listening carefully. The Father continued, "This is a time of great dissension, trials, and testing. Iniquity is abounding as the darkness appears to conquest the light. We will be challenged in unfathomable ways as our hearts will grow weak and weary. We have never experienced an emotional pain of this magnitude, and this will be the first and last time. This one will rival all that is divine, and the darkness within his heart will change the universe in incomprehensible ways – but I will love him no less than the day I created him. You will lead."

Michael's eyes revealed a hint of insecurity, "I'm not sure I can, Father. Maybe you should choose Gabriel or Raphael."

"Raphael is the angel of healing. He cannot lead. Gabriel is my messenger. He cannot lead. You are the closest to me and one of my brightest stars. I shall never leave you nor forsake you. On my command, prepare for battle."

Molech approached Lucifer as he hovered outside of the golden gates of the throne. Lucifer pierced Molech's black eyes. He snarled, "We need an army."

Molech said, "How many?"

Lucifer slowly flew away from the gates as Molech followed, "At least a third of the angels in the heavens."

"Why?"

"We, my brother, are going to overthrow The Father, so we can live on our own accord, according to our own freewill. 'Do as we wilt' will be the whole of the new law. We are rewriting...the beginning as well as the end."

www.ingramcontent.com/pod-product-compliance
Lightning Source LLC
Chambersburg PA
CBHW051723040426
42447CB00008B/947